Brooklyn, New York Business Author
Lisa Rone, MBA
Ollie S. Woods, Ed. S

Marketing Chick

Proven Research for Business Leaders

Library of Congress Number: 2016913953

Disclaimer

The following content shall provide an in depth analysis in the realm of business and leadership. This analytical data shall be coupled with facets of marketing, advertising, and promotions. The author and/or publishers shall not be liable for any miscommunication, damages, poor performance, and/or allegations linked to this content. This reading material is merely an educational guide for ideas, concepts, strategies, and techniques for learning purposes

Dedication

This book is written with affection and gratitude to my husband Christopher for your support and commitment to our family.

And to my two children, Sheba and Shakeel for allowing me to consummate my endeavor as author.

Lisa Rone, MBA

Acknowledgments

We take this opportunity to express our deepest gratitude to our professors at Morris Brown College located in Atlanta, Georgia and to the TRIO program and our former colleagues who supported us with constant encouragement and feeding our hungry souls through the years.

Lastly, we thank God almighty, our parents, brothers, and sisters, and close friends for their constant support and encouragement with this foundation these accomplishments would not be possible.

Lisa Rone, MBA

Ollie Wood, Ed. S

Table of Contents

Dedication iii

Acknowledgments v

TEACHING AND CONSULTING 1

Introduction 3

Chapter 1: Have a Plan 5

Chapter 2: Aggressively Market Services 7

Chapter 3: Monitor Billing 9

Chapter 4: Manage Compliance Issues 11

Chapter 5: Expand Consulting Networks and Relationships 13

Chapter 6: Mentor consultants 15

Chapter 7: Improve Consulting Communication Skills 17

Chapter 8: Build a Character 19

Chapter 9: Update Consulting Competencies 21

Conclusion 23

Essential Questions 25

LEADERSHIP STRATEGIES 35

Leadership Strategies 37

Essential Questions 45

TEAM WORK FOR BUILDING 51
Team Work 53
Strategies for Career Advancement 55
Essential Questions 67

PERFORMANCE MANAGEMENT 75
Performance Management A Leadership and Management Blueprint 77
Essential Questions 89

Book Quotes 97
About the Authors 99
References 101
Puzzles 108

TEACHING AND CONSULTING

Helping You Succeed

Introduction

Consultancy entails the provision of objective and expert advice to businesses so to enable them improve in terms of structure, management, operational capacity, and strategy. The role of consultants in enhancing business growth continues to grow by the day as more and more organizations find themselves seeking specialist expertise on matters relating to organizational productivity. It is for this reason that the consulting industry ranks among the most vibrant and constantly changing economic sectors. The growth of the industry has witnessed more learners aspire to become consultants and young graduates aspire to build successful careers. One major challenge to these individuals is how to attain excellence. Raw consultants aspiring to attain the highest level of professionalism and experience as far as consultancy is concerned strive to reach success and attain financial stability. Of course, reaching success remains a daunting endeavor for a considerable lot considering the increasingly competitive nature of the consulting industry both in the U.S and globally. A typical beginner attempting to establish a foothold in the attractive field of interest is met with challenges not limited to need to possess work experience and pressure to work under training schemes formulated by employers (Sadler, P., 2002). More so, new graduates seeking to enter the consulting market are met with the challenge of beginning to create commercial credibility for marketability; a task exceedingly tough to execute given clients changing needs and overall industry volatility. These challenges make it hard for individuals to establish fast-track careers. This essay examines strategies that can be applied in building successful consultancy careers and elevating graduates to refined financial statuses. A major assumption adopted is that strategy is the key to gainful employment and a rewarding consulting career. It is expected that an exposure of the already applied and proven strategies will help ease the entry process through bridging the gap between raw talent and the market. It is important to note that the strategies proposed are based on successful consultants' recommendations.

Chapter 1:
Have a Plan

The first strategic move towards a successful consulting career is to formulate and adhere to a plan. In order to eliminate the challenges typical of independent consulting, it is important to have a plan that details one's long terms objectives and mechanisms for achieving them. Any consultant ought to have a set of goals. The goals determine the regions of operation, services to be rendered, and target markets. Having a plan sees to it that the new graduate works towards achieving preset goals consequently reducing risk of failure. A plan also ensures that the new entrant in to the consulting profession has a vision, set of values, and mission. Vision and mission are crucial guiding frameworks that bring about direction and purpose. A new graduate with a mission to develop team-based organizations through provision of a variety of consulting services is less likely to fail as they have a plan that affords them direction and purpose. Having a plan is an increasingly important strategy for advancing in the consulting profession. A plan serves as the first indication for determining if a move towards consultancy will be lucrative in future. A plan helps with ascertaining whether one is indeed cut out for a consulting career. Planning allows individuals to make out if their preferences, values, goals, and ambitions are suited for the tasking profession.

Chapter 2:
Aggressively Market Services

An ability to attract new clientele and retail old ones is characteristic of any successful consulting business. As such, it is important that any graduate intending to pursue independent consulting as a career to work towards attracting and holding clients. Inability to attract clients means no business. A good strategy for attracting new customers is to market one's consulting services. While this may seem easy, the actual marketing process is particularly difficult considering marketing consulting services entails convincing customers that they need the services (Webb, J., 2008). Key marketing techniques other than use of main stream media and the internet proposed by consultants getting work include;

- Using brochures- Brochures are effective for communicating service rendered and informing why one is a cut above the competition.

- Cold calling- the new graduate ought to make cold calling work to his advantage. Preparing scripts in advance, integrating creative efforts to convince customers, and limiting the number of cold calls are suggested way to make cold calling work.
- Relying on word-of mouth- Recommendations are an excellent way to gain new customers. Referrals also form a good advertising option for new consultants as it exposes them to prospective clients.
- Public speaking- Public speaking helps build one's image in the society and is an excellent way for a new consultants to put together a positive reputation and generate new clients from it.

Customer attraction and retention is an unending process especially in consulting because it is a pipeline trade. Pursuing a client involves proposing, entering in to an agreement, and consequently, service provision. Therefore, it is important for fresh graduates entering the consulting industry to never stop marketing themselves as only through continuous marketing will they attract new business and maintain old ones.

Chapter 3:
Monitor Billing

Similar to any industry, consulting considers cash as the most essential aspect of existence. To that end, it is important that new consultants monitor their billing and collect their fees to meet the cash flow needs of the start up or up-and-coming entity. Developing routine practices of following up to ensure that payment is received is one way new consultants can ease the billing and collection process. Another way to effectively monitor billing is through maintain lucid communication with clients on matters relating to fees for service rendered. For instance, while gathering information relating to client satisfaction, one can bring in the subject of payment and in so doing, ensure that both parties are on the same page as far as payment goes. It is important to establish close relations with the newly acquired clientele as this helps ease the billing process as well.

Chapter 4:
Manage Compliance Issues

For the new graduate entering the consulting industry, it is important to deliberate on the regulatory requirements and compliance issues and never ignore them. Consulting parallels law in various ways. Talking to legal practitioners and professionals in other fields can help one understand the intricacies involved and the obligations one is expected to meet. More so, it is crucial that the new consultant establishing procedures that ensure compliance with filing and payment requirements. Ignorance of compliance issues may lead to huge financial obligations or huge legal consequences that may call for dissolution (Patti, P. and Jack J., 2004).

Chapter 5:
Expand Consulting Networks and Relationships

To survive in the consulting industry, it is vital to keep on expanding one's contacts. Growing the number of people one knows is just as important as increasing the number of people that know of you and the consultancy. The more people know you and vice versa, the healthier the consultancy. A new entrant will need to stay active on matters relating to business and use such information to develop industry beneficial industry ties (Newton, R., 2012).

Chapter 6:
Mentor consultants

Mentoring consultants with less experience is one way of growing one's consulting business. As the new graduate gains more understanding other industry, he/she should resolve to train those with less experience. As the workload increases, there will be need to recruit other fresh graduates lest one risks accumulating too much work and failing to deliver. Training and mentoring allows for continuity especially when work begins to become too much for one person.

Chapter 7:
Improve Consulting Communication Skills

Communication plays a major role in the consulting profession. Consulting is the means through which relationships are formed. Excellent communications is, therefore, vital from the beginning as it allows for continuous business interactions. Adding to one's consulting communication skills helps the budding consultant to understand their weaknesses and strengths. As a result, the individual faces less and less problems promoting himself/herself over time. Typically, increasing one's communication skill set provides an avenue for raising awareness .

Chapter 8:
Build a Character

Character complements reputation in the consulting industry. The best reputation can easily be eroded if a person's character is wanting. Making character count in the consulting industry is especially important for the new graduate as it helps delineate oneself from others. Building a character entails developing a service-oriented mind that allows for understanding customers' needs and preferences. Newton (2012) notes that character helps with attracting new business particularly during times of low demand

Chapter 9:
Update Consulting Competencies

Consulting requires an individual with a intellectual curiosity. Intellectual curiosity can help new consultants find simple solutions to problems and convey the same to clients. Also, by simply continuously learning, a consultant can keep abreast with trends in the industry and thus be better equipped in terms of skill and abilities. The new graduate will have to actively engage in distant learning programs, participate in seminars, and acquire training materials pertinent to his specialty so as maintain up-to-date competencies that afford him or her some form of competitive edge.

Conclusion

Consulting is an increasingly rewarding profession and is arguably one of the most lucrative careers one can pursue. Not only is it rewarding in terms finance but also in terms of personal satisfaction. It has a number of benefits including becoming one's boss hence the growing interest to pursue it among learners. However, setting a foothold in the industry is exceedingly difficult due to the competitive nature of the sector. Nonetheless, it is possible for the new graduate aspiring to make it in the industry. By simply integrating a set of strategies not limited to having a plan, aggressively marketing services offered, and consistently updating consulting competencies, one can progressively grow and become successful at it.

Essential Questions

Here are some questions that you should be able to answer based off the data provided throughout this case study. Note these essential questions were supported through proven research and development.

- How can you recognize productivity?

- What are some strategies you learned from the reading?

- How would you describe the framework for consulting?

- How would you summarize marketing services?

- What are your thoughts about key marketing techniques used in consultancy?

- How would you apply what you have learned to developing an action plan?

- What is your understanding of client retention?

- What facts would you select to support consultancy?

- Write three to five paragraphs that support promotion of teaching and consulting.

LEADERSHIP STRATEGIES

Stepping Into Your Destiny

Library of Congress Control Number: 2016913468

Leadership Strategies

Employment in the United States is a very sensitive and dire problem. The unemployment rate has been at an all-time high since the economic crunch. People in all sectors of the job market were severely affected by the breakdown of economic structures. People had to rethink strategies and ways in which to succeed in their fields. Companies which were previously trading in the stock markets were rendered bankrupt and had to shut down. There was a massive overthrow of the job market as people lost their jobs, their homes, their livelihoods. The description of a consultant basically- shows the clients the best way to invest their money. It is achieved through choosing wise investments to help secure their future. At the same time, wealth consultants are able to detect patterns of markets and see which investments are good and which are not. In the current work environment, rethinking strategies previously used is very important. There are ways in which people applied for jobs and how they maintained their jobs and prospected for other opportunities. However, these strategies do not work in the current economy.

The first method of success is **self-awareness** (George, 2010). It earns that one is comfortable in own skin and I aware of their abilities and their value. When a person is either applying for a job or prospecting for investments, there are certain modes of communication that one can use that show that one is confident in his/her abilities. The main key to confidence is having proper posture and having the knowledge needed in that specific field. In this case, when one is combated with questions about that field he/she able to answer from the experiences. A person who has confident is aware that a challenge is not a setback but an opportunity to learn and grow (Goleman, 1998).

Assertiveness is the second key to having better chances in the job market. It means that a person will not be turned down by an employer and walk away hurt or offended. Assertive people have the capacity to get negative responses from very many places and still go to the next location and ask for a job. They understand that to find job they may have to knock on more than one door. In the case of looking into investments, assertive people may lose money in the process of investing, but they keep looking for other areas to invest and grow. Assertive people understand the power of learning from past mistakes and growing from every experience (Miltenberger, 2004).

People bondage is the main factor in the gaining and retention of jobs. Bondage in the job environment is when a person is holding onto modes of working business that were used previously. When a person is stuck in a mindset of running the work environments as they were previously done, he/she sets a president to fail in the future. People are also bond in the work environments by others for example, teenagers are affected by peer pressure, and in the same way, and adults are more often disabled in their thought patterns by other people (Kennedy, 1995). The difference between the two forms of bondage is that the person who is bound by other people has a better chance of attaining help than the other one. When one comes to the realization of the abilities, he/she breaks away from all forms of bondage.

Hard skills refer to the set of job abilities that one is able to undertake in a certain work environment. Hard skills more often refer to the amount of workload that one can manage to comfortably do and use it effectively (Kennedy, 1995). In the interview process, one is more often required to prove that he/she has the experience that he/she has stated in the resume. In the financial field, investors are required to have skills in accounting applications and people management skills. Soft skills refer to the capabilities that one is able to do for the company in terms of critical thinking, drafting proposals, and seeing plans through. In the current work environment, one needs a stable balance between the soft and hard skills in order to succeed. By understanding the job market one is able to determine the set of skills he/she needs in order to have a cutting edge above the rest of the employable people in the job market.

Moreover, relationship in the workplace are very sensitive, and one needs to be able to have the capability to deal with them (Miltenberger, 2004). Relationships in the work environment refer to dealing with the superiors, colleagues, and juniors. In the case of dealing with superiors, one has to deal respectfully with them. The respect is required because they have the authority and once one is willing to adapt to the rules and regulations set, they are able to settle a proper working environment with them (Griffin & Ebert, 2010). In the case of colleagues, one needs to learn to be a proper team player in order to live in peace. Once a whole team is able to live in the working environment peacefully, they are more productive. The main factor to success and productivity in this equation is to have good healthy work relationships.

Social responsibility has proven to be a way for the corporate world to reach out into the community. Its acts could range from cleaning up a neighborhood, feeding homeless people and building schools to helping empower the community. Givers and takers in any economy refer to the people who run businesses and those that are on the receiving end. The givers more often have the power over the takers. In the case of employees, one has to truly understand the balance between the two in order to achieve success.

Adaptability in the world of business means how one is able to respond and change in accordance to the surrounding environments. When one is able to adapt to the rules and regulations set in the work environment and in the business world, he/she is able to steer through the different challenges that he/she may face.

Flexibility, in this case, shows he extent to which one is willing to go for their job. Being flexible more often than not means having to deal with longer working hours, giving time and resources in order to succeed. Optimism is a vital part of success in any venture. When one have a positive attitude towards the future, he/she able to look forward to working. The attitude makes it easier to handle more tasks and accomplish more assigned duties. Reality testing in any company is the ability to look at work and resources from an objective angle. From the inside angle of any job, it is possible to be blinded by the running of the company, however, when one takes an objective view they are able to adjust appropriately to the required standards. When one is able to follow through with the Proven Employment Strategies above, it becomes easier to familiarize yourself with the running of the employment world (Doughty & Long, 2009).

Conflict resolution is one of the main reasons why people retain or lose their jobs. There are different kinds of conflict in the working environment. The main reason for conflict in the work environment is a personal conflict between employees. When systems have been put in place to ensure that employees are able to resolve issues without getting out of hand they are able to have better results in the workplace (Griffiths, 2008). However, without proper systems for conflict resolution, the systems fail the employees and the entire running of the business. For an employee to avoid being in trouble with the management, they need to understand to leave personal lives from the work environment. They also need to have an insatiable drive to work diligently for their employers.

Returns in any work environment always come as a result, of working at something consistently. Consistency in any job means sticking through even when things do not work as expected. Having the patience to work and remain focused until you finally succeed at what you are doing. In this economic crunch, only the people who are diligent enough will succeed. Business strategies play a vital role in the growth of any company. These strategies if well implemented ensure success.

Essential Questions

Note: these essential questions were supported through proven research and development.

- **List five proven strategies to becoming a successful consultant.**

- **What is the first method of success?**

- How would you summarize people bondage?

- How are hard skills related to consulting?

- What are your perspectives on social responsibility?

- **Outline an expository draft about the text content.**

TEAM WORK
FOR BUILDING

A Collaboration Guide

Library of Congress Control Number: 2016913467

Team Work

Employees often desire to advance in their careers. For those who join organizations in entry-level positions, they always work hard to ensure that they progress to top leadership ranks. They want to learn new skills and strategies to advance in their careers. Climbing the career ladder comes with additional benefits such as financial increase and high expectations. In light of this, team building is central to ensuring that employees give their best in the workplace. It encourages them to work smart and not just hard with intent to deliver the best results (Dianna, 2006). When employees work in teams, they are more likely to achieve greater success than when they work alone. Teamwork contributes toward building trust among staff members and their motivation. It offers open communication and, consequently, enhances cooperation among employees. The value of team building is more important for individuals who work as wealthy consultants and teachers.

As employees, they need to grow in their personal and professional life. They can achieve it collaborating with their colleagues. Team building aims to improve problem-solving skills as individual members work together to develop sound solutions (Klein, DiazGranados, Salas, Le, Burke, & Goodwin, 2009). Effective teams necessitate diversity, integrity, and dynamics. Further, team building requires companies to use incentives to reward and recognize good performance. Rewards motivate individuals to work hard towards the attainment of shared objectives. In any team building exercise, monitoring and evaluating progress play a crucial role. It makes it possible to determine whether the strategies or activities incline with the stated objectives. Team building purposes are critical for consultants and teachers seeking to advance in their careers.

Strategies for Career Advancement

Problem Solving

Problem solving is one of the main reasons that teams are created. Delegating problem solving allows team members to come up with creative solutions. They brainstorm ideas about the problem, evaluate each of the alternative solutions, and adopt the most effective ones (Tinuke, 2013). For consultants and teachers, they often encounter challenging tasks, which require that they involve their colleagues to find the right decisions. In essence, working alone may appear difficult, especially when the problem is complex. They need to work as teams to solve clients' problems and ensure their satisfaction. More importantly, problem-solving skills increase the ability of team members and help them advance their careers. They can take up more challenging tasks due to their ability to solve problems.

Recruitment

Acquiring and retaining talented employees is critical to the success of any organization. Due the increasingly competitive business environment and growing diversity of available skills, recruiters need to be selective in their recruitment decisions. The need to choose the recruitment method carefully inclines to the fact that poor recruitment decision can have long-term adverse impacts on the organization (Wilson, 1996). Some of the negative effects may include high training, development costs, and high employee turnover. Successful recruitment allows an organization to access a qualified pool of candidates to fill various vacancies. It begins with proper planning and forecasting where an organization formulates the plan to eliminate or fill job openings based on future needs, available talents, and current resources. Recruitment can be done internally through promotions and transfer or via referrals by friends, family members, or staff. In internal recruitment, organizations advertise job openings through posting. Organizations can also recruit through external sources of advertising vacancies in the print media and TV, walk-in applicants, job fairs, or online. The choice of recruitment approach that companies use depends on the job specification and available resources. Overall, effective recruitment is the cornerstone of building efficient teams. It makes it possible for an organization to access talented employees and the right balance of individuals.

Diversity

Diversity involves empowering and involving different groups to achieve a shared objective. It brings together people from diverse backgrounds, knowledge, and experience, and consequently, it improves their capability to resolve problems. Indeed, embracing diversity serves as the first step in building teams. It is worth noting that variety does not just concern about race or gender, but rather, it involves numerous aspects including an intellectual ability that allows enriching teamwork. Diversity gives team members an opportunity to understand and recognize individual differences as the source of strength. It makes it possible for members to comprehend the unique role and value of each person. It allows greater interaction with individuals from different backgrounds, which ultimately contributes towards personal and professional development.

Group Dynamics

Group members have their life experiences and personal histories, vision, aims, knowledge and skills, as well as interests and needs. The interactions between individuals in a group setting are collectively known as group dynamics (Tarricone & Luca, 2002). Team roles are mainly determined by a combination of a person's experience and personality. A confident individual is likely to provide more options while an impatient one can push the discussion ahead. A shy person is more likely to refrain from participating in the group. Considering that team dynamic relies on the relationships among those involved, it is courteous and sensible to introduce members to each other and provide them with opportunities to build relationships. Proper management of group dynamics is critical to ensuring that teams work together (LaFasto & Larson, 2001). For consultants and teachers, they work with different people from diverse backgrounds, which require that they know each other and aim towards improving their performance and, ultimately, careers.

Integrity

Integrity entails doing the right thing regardless of whether someone is watching. It is about being honest. Integrity is a requirement for building effective teams. It provides a foundation for building trust and relationships among team members (Klein, et al., 2009). It makes it possible for individuals to concentrate on their tasks without worrying about the consequences of their actions so long as they are doing the right things. Integrity implies that group members cannot comprise their values and principles. It helps build effective teams as individuals commit themselves to execute their respective roles. Integrity is of particular importance as it makes individuals credible and trustworthy. In essence, such a person can be entrusted with important responsibilities, which ultimately aid in career advancement. Of course, as one ascends the career path, he or she assumes leadership roles in the organization. The position comes with a heavy responsibility of making critical decisions that require the person to have a sound character.

Incentives

Incentives play a vital role in building teams. They can be either monetary or non-monetary such as recognition and praise that motivate employees to double their efforts to succeed (Wilson, 1996). When workers feel valued and recognized for their contribution in the workplace, they are more likely to increase their efforts. It is natural that no one acts without having a purpose of being driven by something. Therefore, rewards act as a stimulus for individuals to improve their performance (McKnight, Ahmad, & Schroeder, 2001). When incentives are given to groups or teams, they play a vital function in building team cohesion and trust. It allows employees to work as a team towards achieving a shared goal.

Mindless Activities

Mindless activities provide an opportunity for team members to interact with each other and build strong relationships. By their very nature, such activities allow individuals to participate without any specific purpose or goal to accomplish. They do not require thoughts to complete and act as a mental break, allowing team members to refresh, re-energize, and help generate new ideas (Kets, 1999). Although they require little attention, such tasks demand adequate time. The activities are productive as they build strong teams by providing a chance for members to learn about each other. Moreover, they improve individual skills and knowledge, which aid in career growth. Some of the examples include removing the crap on the working table, raking the yard, among others. Mindless activities rely on one's habits to accomplish them while doing or consuming another productive thing.

Proper Communication

Effective communication is central to the success of teams. It creates a workplace environment where problem-solving and creative ideas are encouraged (Harvey, Millet, Smith, 1998). Proper communication helps in building trust among team members; it reduces the chances of conflicts. Moreover, the individuals can understand the overall goals and ensure that they understand each other and develop positive relationships. Effective communication helps clarify any doubts about certain issues and allows team members to work in an environment where they have access to information. Team members should be willing to receive and give constructive criticisms and provide accurate feedback (Tarricone & Luca, 2002).

Monitoring the Progress

Team building is a process of changing a group into a team by setting goals, clarifying roles, allocating resources, monitoring progress, and rewarding for achievements (LaFasto & Larson, 2001). It comes out that for effective team building to occur, proper monitoring of the progress is critical. Monitoring and reviewing the progress of individuals and teams as a whole make it possible to identify successes and areas that need further improvement. It allows team members to determine whether their actions incline with the set goals and objectives.

Evaluation

The evaluation goes beyond monitoring to identify ways in which implementation progress can be strengthened to overcome identified weaknesses (Klein, et al., 2009). It should be carried out regularly on a weekly or monthly basis to keep track of the progress and ensure that it does not deviate from the set objectives. In essence, evaluation is conducted based on the performance goals. It helps the team to make changes accordingly to achieve high performance.

Proven Employment Strategies

Employment strategies aim to increase access to job opportunities, remove existing barriers, and assist in retaining and attracting skilled personnel from a diverse background. The first strategy is advertising job vacancies through the print and TV media to reach many potential candidates. In addition, the recruitment should involve job fairs and referrals. To retain employees, organizations must provide good remuneration package that includes reasonable pay and other benefits (Dianna, 2006). Besides, mentoring and coaching programs are necessary to equip workers with skills required for them to perform their duties. Above all, introducing flexible working to support work-life balance plays a critical role in retaining staff members.

Challenges of Team Building

Although team-building strategies support career advancement, they have certain limitations. Challenges of the teams begin with group members' attempt to replace individualized work. Rewarding teams can lead to intra-team conflict as members can begin to compete for attention and recognition for their accomplishment as opposed to cooperating to achieve bigger organization goals (Wageman, 1997). It is important to figure out ways of rewarding teamwork in a manner that encourages cooperation. A team building strategy of using mindless activities can consume a lot of time, which otherwise, would be spent on productive activities. Meaningless and mindless activities may create unnecessary tensions between employees and reduce their motivation or satisfaction with their work. Staff members that have immense technical knowledge like completing their tasks individually often find difficulties interacting with team members. Instead of building strong relationships and trust, inappropriate social relations may distract team members from accomplishing their task (Kets, 1999). Team-building activities can lead to an unprofessional and overly casual approach in the workplace. Therefore, team building can undermine the main objective of ensuring effective communication among team members.

In summary, the case study has examined the ways in which team building strategies can help in career growth and financial increase of consultants and teachers. Teaming building aims to ensure sound leadership skills, positive communication, and the ability to work closely to resolve problems. It provides opportunities for employees to interact with each other and build strong relationships that are necessary for high performance. They work together to solve problems that arise in the workplace. However, the success of teams depends on their integrity, group dynamics, and diversity. The three factors must be considered when developing strong teams. Further, it is important that employers use incentives to reward good performance and motivate them to double their efforts. Effective communication facilitates positive interaction between team members and helps clarify any issues that may arise. Importantly, monitoring progress provides a way in which teams can determine the success and weaknesses of their activities. Accordingly, they can develop intervention measures to avoid deviation from the set objectives. Although team-building strategies have certain limitations, they provide an opportunity for individuals to advance in their careers.

Essential Questions

Note: These essential questions were supported through proven research and development.

- **How can you resolve delegation problems?**

- How can you off-set poor recruitment methods?

- How is diversity related to team building?

- What facts would you select to support group dynamics?

- Why is integrity important for building an effective team?

- What are non-monetary incentives and how are they used in the workplace?

- Should team work theories be banned in all entry-level positions?

- Write three to five paragraphs that support collaboration?

PERFORMANCE MANAGEMENT

A Leadership and Management Blueprint

Library of Congress Control Number: 2016913466

Performance Management

A Leadership and Management Blueprint

Organization should strive to employ strategies that are maximizing effectiveness in its operation without damaging its competence or culture. An organization should employ advanced technology to improve its productivity which ultimately creates a wide market share. E-business model is a strategy that promotes an organizational marketing approach. Leadership in an organization should use strategies that help to identify talents, develop as well as retain them. Organization should employ the culture of motivating workers by rewarding and recognizing the best performers that indirectly promote customer satisfaction and a win over a wide market share. The management should enhance their competitive advantage through positive publicity such as charitable activities involvement. Recruitment and selection strategy helps to get suitable professions that led to the profitability potential of the organization.

Significantly, the performance management strategy results in hardworking employees since they want to produce appealing working results. This paper seeks to discuss the most sustainable strategies for organizational competencies.

Organization should endeavor to comply with the most advanced technology in order to compete favorably with other firms in the industry. This will significantly help to raise high returns on investments. In this regard, an organization should be capable of effectively manage change whenever necessary. Therefore, the leaders and management should employ a strategic approach to facilitating change that will optimally effective the profitability potential of the organization (Ahuja & Khamba, 2008). Change in an organization is associated with various elements including effective communication, training, personal counseling and implementation monitoring. Firstly, change requires an advance communication to the entire workforce concerning the necessity for the adjustment. Also, the management requires establishing a change plan to ensure a systematic implementation. Secondly, it is essential for employees to adapt and understand the change via an effective training and education. This is because the new process and the related skills are unfamiliar to the employees and they have to learn to adapt to the new daily workflow (Akrivos, Ladkin & Reklitis, 2007). Thirdly, there should be personal counseling department such as the human resource to help the employees who may feel uncomfortable to about the change. Finally, the management should monitor the flow of change in the organization. This should be done through statistical data that can help to compare the previous and current performance. Similarly, it should monitor how the overall production progression is fairing with the change. Management should fine-tune on change strategy to ensure its success whenever the change is not effective compared to the previous process. Therefore, organization change is a crucial strategy to ensure it suits the current market requirements as well as improve the efficiency of the firm.

The e-commerce business model is a strategy that promotes an organization marketing approach. It enhances the buying and selling part of the business via internet orders. Apparently, e-commerce is a convenient strategy that enables an organization to penetrate into the international market. Additionally, the customer relationship is promoted since the internet options particularly the social media platform as well as the website allows to hold a conversation (Beckhard, 1969). Initiating an effective communication to the clients will boost the customer relationship. As a result, the organization can gain a wide market share which eventually results in profitability. On the contrary, the e-business strategy is connected to supply chain expenditures. These are business act ivies that are worth practicing since there lays a higher return on investments (Belleflamme & Peitz, 2015). Furthermore, fewer organizations will take part in the kind of business sectors which lowers the competition range. Supply chain activities enhance the organization competencies, sustainability, timing, appropriability, and opportunism. However, the internet strategy is a hypercompetitive business environment which requires the organization to effectively use its resources to obtain a competitive advantage. In this regard, it is important to establish a dynamic resources model in order to effortlessly ascertain and allocate resources.

It is essential for management to identify, develop and retain talents in an organization. This will involve direct supervision during working sessions and teamwork approaches. Besides, job rotation and motivation of employees can help to identify talents which basis the organizational prosperity (Matarasso &Smith, 2015). In this regard, talent management system should be employed as well as training the leaders and manage the better methods of identifying talents. This will eventually boost the productivity of different departments of the organization which is the basis for its entire success. Significantly, visionary leaders are focused on updating existing talents through training and motivation approaches. These leaders endeavor to develop, manage talent with heavy investments. As a result, a strong culture characterized by high-performing teamwork, accountability, and qualified resources (Raisch & Foreword, 2000). Also, it helps to improve HR and entire organizational effectiveness. Therefore, leaders should employ talent identification strategy and team working culture that helps to acquire current business needs.

Positive publicity is a business strategy that influences the business reputation resulting in competitive advantage. A positive reputation of an organization in the market contributes to the brand loyalty. Apparently, publicity and advertisements are focused on promoting the overall competitive advantage of the organization in the market (Ritter, 2016). However, publicity comprises of activities such as involvement in charitable events. This indicates that donating time and talents is a business developmental strategy. Additionally, organizations should engage in charitable activities that comply with its line of duty and utilizes their unique skills. Many charitable events involvement will provide a platform where the organization can meet a large variety of clients. However, fewer charitable activities are effective because it will help to capture and retain consumer's who are easily manageable. Significantly, an organizational magazine or brochure featuring the charitable events is more meaningful to clients (Sheldon, 1991). This is a strategy of gaining loyalty and building a stronger relationship with customers in the market. Therefore, the organization should endeavor to be involved in charitable activities that help to create a positive reputation in the market as well as a stronger relationship with the prospective customers.

Management should use the recruitment and selection strategy that helps to hire the suitable personnel for the existing job. This should be done by forecasting the kind of jobs that will be available in future to be able to understand their positions and duties to undertake (Ahuja & Khamba, 2008). In this case, management should record the outlined positions and create a targeted recruiting plan which includes responsibilities, knowledge, competencies, relevant skills and cultural fit identifying process. In order to find the person with top qualifications, the organization should use creative and current recruiting sources such as the social media platform (Beckhard, 1969). Meanwhile, the recruitment strategy that allows the management, organization and the candidate to learn about each other is significantly the best approach.

The management should also use the performance management strategy for each employee. This will drive employees to work extra hard to give appealing results. Indeed, it allows feedback and space for improvement to the employees as well as motivation to the workers who have done extremely well (Ritter, 2016). On the other hand, the strategy manages problem performers and increases compensations and bonuses to employees as a result, of the company performance. However, the management should establish an individual development plan for the poor performers to ensure their frequent monitoring. If the problem performer does not achieve the expectations no matters the opportunity and tools he or she has been granted to facilitate his improvement, it is wise to eliminate them. This is because they may affect the rest of the team which can result in resources drain as well as huge amount of losses (Sheldon, 1991). Therefore, the management should attempt to employ a performance management strategy that motivates the employees as well as help to identify poor performing workers.

Significantly, employee's engagement is a strategy that management should endeavor to employ to boost the workers satisfaction. The engagement should involve decision making as well as early communication on a certain concept. Evidently, communication is effective for transparency since the employees want to know the organizational ability to pay salaries on time (Belleflamme & Peitz, 2015). Also, the workers need to know the worthiness of their work to provide bonuses or salaries increase. Additionally, conducting an employee contentment survey should ensure that questions are carefully designed to get comprehension on the themes that are critical to the organization. The feedback method should be anonymous to ensure that they feel comfortable, thereby, giving honest response concerning their feelings. The leadership team should synthesize the data and conduct a feedback session with the workers. This will help to establish an action plan to those dissatisfied. Therefore, the employee's engagement strategy helps to identify the unsatisfied individuals (Ritter, 2016). Besides, the management should endeavor to celebrate jobs things that employees love in an aim to establish overall satisfaction for greater performance.

By rewarding and recognizing employees who provide the best performance helps in boosting the morale of the workforce. In fact, it demonstrates appreciation for the contributions toward the success of the organization (Sheldon, 1991). Also, it promotes productivity of individual and group performance. Obviously, happy employees will provide quality services to customers enhancing the customer relationship as well as establishing their loyalty. Moreover, it improves the customer satisfaction, internal moral and ethics compliance as well as preventing turnover. Rewarding should incorporate birthday and anniversaries acknowledgment. Also, end of year bonuses, tea break, and fun Friday refreshments should be included. Additionally, the rewarding employee is a strategy for retaining employees as well as training new ones (Matarasso & Smith, 2015). This significantly helps to decrease the long-term training cost. Evidently, rewarded employees go an extra mile and are productive with greater loyalty as well as eager to contribute to the firm in a meaningful and impactful way. Therefore, it is essential for management in an organization to recognize and reward employees to establish a workplace morale that results in the overall prosperity of the firm.

Effective HRM is a strategy that helps to achieve an organizational mission, vision, and goals. Consequently, the HRM personnel should consist of professional experts to be able to achieve competence. They should be able to recognize the direct association between programs, procedure, policies and services they compromise and the organizational purpose. The Chief HRM officers should implement strategic approach into work which begins with thinking before performing. In fact, they should endeavor to comply with the HR philosophies and policies. Besides, they should have a serving and help mindset that influences organization, staffing, and operation (Raisch & Foreword, 2000). Ultimately, the HRM officers should leverage human potential on behalf of the entire firm in order for it to achieve its goals and objectives. In this regard, the officials should not be biased to employees alone; instead, they should work for the better of the organization. Indeed, they should develop, support, encourage and enable employees in building capacity for the better of the firm. Besides, the department should empower, enable and engage the workforce for the welfare of the organization endeavors

(Akrivos, Ladkin & Reklitis, 2007). Therefore, the HRM department has a crucial role finding, developing, managing and nurturing talents in an organization to ensure its growth and development.

Conclusively, performance management is a crucial element in aligning and mobilizing the entire organization to reach higher productivity as well as collaborate to deliver results. The technological advances ease the performance management per individual employee thereby helping to trace poor workers in an organization. Similarly, the technology has greatly promoted the e-commerce in the current organization. This marketing strategy helps to reach a global market for their products. Besides, the internet provides the social media option which enables customer feedback as well as strengthening the relationship between the clients and the organization. Typically, organizations are using publicity techniques to create awareness about the company as well as its products among its prospective and future customers. On the contrary, HRM department is an organizational success-based strategy whose compliance results in organizational competencies. Apparently, the reward system brings morale to hard work thereby influencing higher productivity in the long-run.

Essential Questions

Note: these essential questions were supported through proven research and development.

- **What business model promotes the organization marketing approach?**

- **Describe supply chain activities.**

- Why is it essential for management to identify, develop, and retain talents in their organization?

- How does publicity relate to competitive advantages?

- What facts about charitable events support brand loyalty?

- How should you use performance management strategy?

- **Why is a feedback session coupled with surveys?**

- **Outline three to five paragraphs about human resource management.**

Book Quotes

1. *I choose to be a productive citizen, every time God allows me to breathe.*

    By Lisa Rone, MBA

2. *Have an impact on a situation that will help someone else.*

    By Lisa Rone, MBA

3. *Creative managers use strategies.*

    By Lisa Rone, MBA

4. *As a leader, you must wear your emotions in your shoes—that way those who look up to you can't take you down.*

    By Lisa Rone, MBA

5. *When opportunity didn't knock on my door, I opened my door and snatched opportunity.*

    By Lisa Rone, MBA

6. *Self pride can heal a void.*
    By Lisa Rone, MBA

7. *Good leadership ensures organizational progress.*
    By Lisa Rone, MBA

8. *A Smiling workplace is a key to great collaboration.*
    By Lisa Rone, MBA

9. *Why post when you can publish.*
    By Lisa Rone, MBA

10. *Team Building makes the world rotate.*
    By Lisa Rone, MBA

11. *Good leadership is good management.*
    By Lisa Rone, MBA

12. *Who needs the sun, when you have the SON?*
    By Lisa Rone, MBA

13. *God answered my prayers when HE sent creative Independent Freelancers~* Lisa Rone, MBA

14. *Habits are hard to break so, when you act like a donkey, people tend to TREAT you like a DONKEY.* By Lisa Rone, MBA

About the Authors

Lisa Rone, MBA was born in Brooklyn, New York. She is the second oldest of nine children and is the first among her siblings to earn a college degree. She is committed to research and development, dedicated to her community, and active in her faith.

Ollie Wood, Ed. S served as a wife and mother for over 40 years and acted as a campaign manager in the political career of her husband who served as Atlanta's City Councilman and Fulton County Commissioner. She received the Certificate of Achievement from Morris Brown College through the Upward Bound Program. In the field of mathematics, she has been awarded the Student Support Service award. She has also received the Vital Link award from the National Education Association for recruitment.

References

Ahuja, I. P. S., & Khamba, J. S. (2008). Strategies and success factors for overcoming challenges in TPM implementation in Indian manufacturing industry. *Journal of Quality in Maintenance Engineering, 14*(2), 123-147.

Akrivos, C., Ladkin, A., & Reklitis, P. (2007). Hotel managers' career strategies for success. *International Journal of Contemporary Hospitality Management, 19*(2), 107-119.

Beckhard, R. (1969). Organization development: Strategies and models.

Belleflamme, P., & Peitz, M. (2015). *Industrial organization: markets and strategies*. Cambridge University Press.

Doughty, C. & Long, M. (2009). *Handbook of second language acquisition.* Oxford: Blackwell.

George, E. (2010). The world's biggest employers. *Forbes.*

Goleman, D. (1998). *Working with emotional intelligence.* New York, NY: Bantum Books.

Griffin, R., J. & Ebert, R., W. (2010). *Business essentials (8th ed.).* Upper Saddle River, NJ: Prentice Hall.

Griffiths, C. (2008). *Strategies and good language learners.* In C. Griffiths (Ed.), Lessons from good language learners (pp. 83–98). Cambridge: Cambridge University Press.

Kennedy, E. (1995). Ruling passions. *The New York Times.*

Miltenberger, R. G., (2004). *Behavior modification principles and procedures* (3rd ed). Belmont, CA: Wadsworth/Thomson Learning.Matarasso, A., & Smith, D. M. (2015). Combined breast surgery and abdominoplasty: Strategies for success. *Plastic and reconstructive surgery,135*(5), 849e-860e.

Raisch, W., & Foreword By-Gartner, G. (2000). *The eMarketplace: Strategies for success in B2B eCommerce*. McGraw-Hill Professional.

Ritter, J. (2016). Marketing strategy in the 21st century, a review and assessment of strategies and procedures for success and implementation.*The Business & Management Review, 7*(3), 68.

Serra, C. E. M., & Kunc, M. (2015). Benefits Realisation Management and its influence on project success and on the execution of business strategies.*International Journal of Project Management, 33*(1), 53-66.

Sheldon, B. E. (1991). *Leaders in libraries: Styles and strategies for success.* Chicago: American Library Association.

Newton, R. (2012). *The Management Consultant: Mastering the Art of Consultancy.* London; United Kingdom. Pearson Press.

Patti, P. and Jack J. (2004). *Building a Successful Consulting Practice Opportunities and Challenges.* ROI Institute Inc. Web :> http://www.roiinstitute.net/wp-content/uploads/2014/12/Building-a-Successful-Consulting-Practice.pdf

Sadler, P. (2002). *Management consultancy: A handbook for best practice.* London: Kogan Page.

Webb, J. (2008). *Becoming a Successful Independent Consultant.* Online resource :> http://www.top-consultant.com/articles/becoming%20a%20successful%20independent%20consultant.pdf

Dianna, E. (2006). *Teams: Teamwork and team building.* New York, NY: Prentice Hall.

Harvey, S., Millet, B., & Smith, D. (1998). Developing successful teams in organizations. *Australian Journal of Management & Organizational Behavior, 1*(1), 1-8.

Kets, M.F. (1999). High-performance teams: Lessons from the Pygmies. *Organizational Dynamics, 1* (2), 66-77.

Klein, C., DiazGranados, D., Salas, E., Le, H., Burke, C.S., & Goodwin, F.G. (2009). Does team building work? *Small Group Research, 40* (2), 181-122.

LaFasto, F.M., & Larson, C. (2001). *When teams work best.* Thousand Oaks, CA: Sage.

McKnight, H., Ahmad, S., & Schroeder, R. G. (2001). When do feedback, incentive control, and autonomy improve morale? *Journal of Managerial Issues, 13* (4), 466-470.

Tarricone, P., & Luca, J. (2002). *Successful teamwork: A case study.* Retrieved on May 5, 2016, from: http://www.unice.fr/crookall-cours/teams/docs/team%20Successful%20teamwork.pdf

Tinuke, F.M. (2013). Towards effective team building in the workplace. *International Journal of Education and Research,* 1(4), 1-12.

Wageman, R. (1997). Critical success factors for creating superb self-managing teams. *Organizational Dynamics,* 26 (1), 49-60.

Wilson, F. (1996). Great teams build themselves, team performance management. *An International Journal,* 2 (2), 27-31.

Puzzles

Marketing Sense

```
E M Z A B I N B C B R F K B C
C T S G N I N R A E H O A R K
P V A C K B H L M N O D B C S
I G L D A I A D P E K D Y A T
H L L G I N R N A L N A U U L
S O A P C D M J I Y O C B Q I
D B C E A G N D G T Z I R L D
R A E A R N E A N S A X J T E
A L L O C A T E C E M W I C N
H O S L D U G X S F A M N R T
T S A L G K R N H I E A E P I
N E I E C L E B A L I N A A T
D N K O O B Y A D L N Q C F Y
E F A C T O R F L A E M J Z J
O K D G I H L A B R E L F A E
```

ALLIANCE
BALANCE
CALL
DAYBOOK
EARN
FACTOR
HARDSHIP
LABEL
TIME

ALLOCATE
BANKABLE
CAMPAIGN
DEADLINE
EARNINGS
GLOBAL
HARM
LABOR

AMAZON
BANNER
CANDIDATE
DEAL
FACT
GROSS
IDENTITY
LIFESTYLE

Learn Marketing

```
W P H S V K E Y M C Q T F M K
R I E T Y A O I K A U O A R N
O E T N L E L Z T L A Y M G E
D F R H I A L I L C L X Z A L
O L B A H L E L D U I M T R D
M R O F W O A H U L T N E Z A
X N W O D T L E M A Y P C W T
H S J Y S P F D X T R P N R E
D E P N N M R O I E R U A P J
Q K I B E T R E S N N R L H E
B R A I N E R E C I G M A T I
L A B O L G N H F I R X B A B
C F N Q T T Y O K A S Q V O M
V V W U I K R I L X M E D T O
J U D G E M W A A E E M L H Z
```

ALARM	BALANCE	BRAINER
CALCULATE	DATE	EATN
FORM	GLOBAL	HEALTH
INSTALL	JUDGE	KEY
LINE	MELTDOWN	OATH
PRECISE	QUALITY	REPRESENT
SOFTWARE	TAG	UNIFORM
VALID	WIKI	WITHHOLDING
ZOMBIE		

Business Terms

```
E W T W Z H Q L M T O U U R S
R L W Y A E I L N H H P P O I
U L B C P A L E K Z N S S T G
X N K A M I M D A T E E C A N
W E L E T N C A L C U L A T E
R O W O G I G A G B N L L I R
T U L I A A F B L M N I E L I
Z R L F I D A O A A J N Y I H
I A E N A C I Q R O D G T C F
R O Y L K T O N L P O B I A F
E S A B A T A D G L N N L F E
Q T O E M A G D K O L U I A H
C N M R A L A C B O H A C Q C
E G Z L V B A G G A G E A J A
A Q R X D B C B V U K X F J C
```

ALARM	ALERT	ALIGNMENT
BACKBONE	BACKLOG	BAGGAGE
CACHE	CALCULATE	DATABASE
DATAFLOW	DATE	EMAIL
FACILITATOR	FACILITY	GAIN
GAME	HACKER	HIRE
SIGN	TYPICAL	UNLOADING
UNPROFITABLE	UPSCALE	UPSELLING

Marketing Search

```
E L V P A S Y U P S C A L E N
V C B I U B T X U F K D G A H
V E D Z D F I R E E B D T A E
Y G N S I A R Q U M E I C Z E
P C B T E C G V V L O K E S C
E A I M N T E K W N E R T H I
B L P M C O T O A R O D V S T
L A P E E R N L A T I P A C S
B E N M R K I T I B E D J C U
S T B N A W E L I F M W I O J
U O F A E X O B E C Y T I W F
W U O W L R E R O O C D O O S
Q Q V M G M X O K A A I I R O
O S J H C I F R T R L A E K Z
O B J E C T I V E S O L D W Y
```

AUDIENCE
DEBIT
FILE
JUSTICE
MIC
PAPERWORK
SOLD
VENT
ZIP

BANNER
EXAMPLE
HACKER
KNOWLEDGE
NATIONAL
QUOTE
TACTICS
WORK

CAPITAL
FACTOR
INTEGRITY
LABEL
OBJECTIVE
RADIO
UPSCALE
ZERO

Marketing Folks

```
I V V K S A T E O Y N H K M A
W G O K S N L F T G Q K B L C
D Y I C G I A I Z D H S L E O
S S C A F Y U S Q N I O F R R
J D E B N Q O B D G C J O I B
D E M K E I P Y R A L A S W W
P A A C I J T C T H Q N N S E
P L I I P P I E L B A K N A B
C I L K R V O D R A L L Y T S
C U H O H A N O A A G J E V S
J A F S Z S N C S O Y D N P U
W I L I D I A T P R L J O B B
T H K L N R P W E C Z P M E F
J K P Z A U A U Q L I C U A O
I G O G L Q Q H G R O W T H Q
```

ALLOCATE
DEAL
GROWTH
KICKBACK
NASDAQ
QUERY
TASK
WASH

BANKABLE
EQUITY
HARDSHIP
LAST
OPTION
RALLY
UPLOAD
WIRE

CALL
FILE
JOB
MONEY
PROFIT
SALARY
VOICEMAIL
ZIP

Marketing More

```
T Y L H W J S D Y P O R M I E
N D T I Y K O R O R I R E N C
E E L I F P O I D O N Z M S R
M L T G L T O E N M G E I P O
N A Q A S I R T E T T V T E F
O B I I I E B M H A T O R C O
R O H D U T B I G E K L I T P
I R F L A E O I S V S C A I T
V J A L R M T G J N Y I X O I
N V E S E S G N E I O L S N O
E R H M E T O U Q N N P I J N
T I L V P A C K A G E G S A G
P S N G R E B M O O L B L E D
E I F A I T H S D N O B A E R
C O M P L I A N C E W A G E S
```

AIRTIME
BONDS
ENVIRONMENT
FORCE
HYPOTHESIS
JINGLE
LOVE
NEGOTIATE
PACKAGE
VALUE
ZIP

ALERT
COMPLIANCE
FAITH
GOOD
INSPECTION
JOINT
MEMBERSHIP
OPTION
QUOTE
WAGE

BLOOMBERG
DAILY
FILE
HISTORY
INVESTIGATE
LABOR
MEMO
ORDER
RESPONSIBILITY
WILL

Marketing Matters

```
H F U V A E W K S O R E T T E
A T Z N K U S D B O T J E N D
E I D R O A D J P A L Y C E U
C Q R I T I E I L S T L H M T
A K U X W C T U E N B T N P I
P C C I T D C A I N Y J I O T
A I Y I V E N A T M C E Q L A
C R V U P A T A L I N E U E R
I E O S C R L D B M C W·E V G
T E X P E R I E N C E I S E D
Y M K C R O V M N Q N M L D U
U D N U O P M O C T F N I O E
R U T N E M E E R G A X K T S
V I O Q R S T A T E M E N T N
S E L B A R E V I L E D B G T
```

AGREEMENT
BANDWIDTH
DELIVERABLES
EQUIVALENT
LINE
SOLICITATION
TASK
UNCERTAINTY

AIR
CAPACITY
DEVELOPMENT
EXPERIENCE
OBJECTIVE
SPECULATE
TECHNIQUES

AUDIENCE
COMPOUND
DUE
GRATITUDE
RICK
STATEMENT
TIME

Marketing Buddy

```
E P S D C V A I G V E S W D Q
N F N D A B P N R E S P E C T
E M A N T R I R S O L P M B K
N H T S A L S Z E W O M I V N
Z W S H L V E Z C S E F T X G
G W O E O F N D I H S R Z O I
J Y S N G E I T L A C I H T E
Q P A K K F L C R C O D E L R
U U R W A R E H O U S E A B O
Y O A D V I D E B T Z N S U F
W U I N M E I L A C R I B D G
F S I P T M U P L U J E P G X
O R O U O I G R O D N E V E Z
V R N R G P T J O F F E R T H
T L E U J D Q Y I U Z B M I L
```

ANSWER
CODE
FOREIGN
IMPORT
LABOR
OFFER
RESPECT
UPSELLING
WORK

BUDGET
DEPOSIT
GUIDELINES
JOURNAL
MORE
PRESS
SAFE
VENDOR
ZIP

CATALOG
ETHICAL
HELP
KNOWN
NAME
QUANTITY
TIME
WAREHOUSE

Marketing Partner

```
K G O T M T T L J G L N B Y I
U S O G H A J A M L C R E G M
C G C A G K S S G E Y E H N P
S F E I L E B T Y H X V A I O
E U N I T N O C S I D O V T R
C F R B B Y A M L B E Y I S T
E H O J T M L U E G S R O O K
J Q K R O T X A A C T R R H A
U R U L E U G M N N Q A P N P
D Q P I R S I O U A F C A Y U
J I H Y T D I O L M T L V X O
D F O R M Y M G R A Y N G S R
C I S A B A X D H Z T S E Z G
D I R E C T I V E T J A D V Q
C A R E E R O O T K U T C A E
```

AMOUNT	ANALYTICS	ANALYZE
BASIC	BEHAVIOR	BELIEFS
CAREER	CARRYOVER	CATALOG
DIPLOMACY	DIRECTIVE	DISCONTINUE
EQUITY	EVENT	FORESIGHT
FORM	GOAL	GROUP
HOSTING	IMAGE	IMPORT
LAST	LUXURY	TAG

Mareting World

```
H T N A T L U S N O C E I E Y
N K S E C A S Y T L Y L N D L
H O H E N O G A O G I B T U P
B C I S L O N G F N S A E T P
T J W T L P I T T E S S G I A
E E P O E S M E A E Z O R T E
R I P E T R G A N C M P I A T
H A N I A R C I X U T S T L H
U R C S A A L S R E E I Y Z I
B S E T U E Y O I Q P D P J C
N M I F D R F S B D K F O O A
E O M I F R A M E W O R K F L
N H U Z C U L N B R O W S E R
Y G U E S T B T C I R T S I D
T E G D U B O H J E T M O R O
```

ANSWER
BROWSER
CONSULTANT
DISPOSABLE
EXAMPLES
GUEST
INTEGRATION
LOGISTICS

APOLOGY
BUDGET
CONTACT
DISTRICT
FORUM
GUIDELINES
INTEGRITY
SAFE

APPLY
BUFFER
DISCRETION
ETHICAL
FRAMEWORK
INSURANCE
LATITUDE

Notes

Notes

Notes

Notes

Notes

Notes

Notes